ENDORSEMENTS

I love Jenny Weaver. One night I went on Facebook to do a live "Singing the Scriptures" segment, and as I typed in "Singing the Scriptures," suddenly Jenny Weaver popped up. She was singing the Psalms over people with her guitar, and it was so powerful. I messaged her saying, "I want to meet you." I love telling people that Jenny is my friend. Jenny is fire. Jenny is passion. She is freedom. She is 100 percent sold out to Jesus Christ and His Word—and her testimony rocked my world.

I highly encourage you to read Jenny's brand-new book, *The Sound of Freedom*. She tells her story—an unbelievable walk through the darkest of dark and how God snatched her out and brought her into His marvelous light. This book will encourage you and empower you to believe and receive that what God did in Jenny's life, He will do the same in your life, your family and your children's lives. Your faith will be empowered as you read through this book. Our God is a breakthrough God, and this is Jenny's story. Her testimony impacted me to trust God in every situation—for the darkest, hardest people. I believe her book will you impact you, setting free the most bound of every captive.

JULIE MEYER
Author of *Dreams & Supernatural Encounters,*
and *Singing the Scriptures*
Intotheriver.net, an online worship community
Healing Rooms of Santa Maria Apostolic Center
Santa Maria, CA

Jenny Weaver's backstory in *The Sound of Freedom* substantiates the glory that follows her ministry. She's a walking, living, breathing miracle of authenticity and authority, which is evident when she worships. *The Sound of Freedom* is the result of Jenny Weaver's life of freedom and the freedom she triumphs in sharing her extraordinary testimony with the world.

DR. TRAVIS JENNINGS
Author, *Champions: It's Time to Get in the Ring, Lifeguard: Help Is On the Way, Life on Turbo,* and *Faith for the Gold*

The Sound of Freedom is one of the most transparent, transforming, Jesus-provoking books I've read in years. Although this book is brief, it's filled with treasures that have the ability to grip your heart and believe that with God nothing is impossible. The way Jenny Weaver shares her testimony is heartfelt and authentic. She provides her readers with the truth of who she was in the beginning, and takes us on a journey of who God has always been—faithful. I appreciate the transparency, because it allows the readers to capture the transformation and leave with a sense of hope, that if God did it for Jenny, He will do it for me.

This book is beautifully written; you can feel the realness of Jenny's story, as well as the power of the Holy Spirit working through her life as a child. Oftentimes (one word) people see a worshipper and have no idea why or how the worshipper developed such a freedom and love for Christ. This book explains it all, and demonstrates how, although hell had a plan, God's plan prevailed. *The Sound of Freedom* is a powerful, must-read book that I highly recommend.

SOPHIA RUFFIN
Founder of Sophia Ruffin Ministries
Author of *Set Free and Delivered*

Jenny Weaver has a breathtaking story of God's love and redemptive power. Not only is this book inspiring and filled with hope, but her life is infused with revival and power! God has used Jenny to sing His songs of freedom over people and nations. This book will release liberty and breakthrough in your life.

RYAN LESTRANGE
Founder of TRIBE, iHubs Movement, RLM
Author of *Hell's Toxic Trio*

Jenny Weaver is an emerging pioneer carrying a sound that has been birthed in the fires of trial and triumph. Her testimony and story will soften the hardest of hearts and awaken a generation to the compassion and tenderness of our loving heavenly Father. This book will give you hope and confidence that God indeed is the God of restoration and that He is plucking brands from the fire like Jenny and raising them up as firebrands for such a time as this. As you will soon discover, Jenny Weaver not only carries a song and message, her life and story are the song and message. Let the firebrands arise!

JEREMIAH JOHNSON
Jeremiah Johnson Ministries

In *The Sound of Freedom*, prophetic revivalist and worshipper Jenny Weaver shares lifelong lessons and imparts wisdom keys through the lens of transparency of her own life and testimony that will revolutionize the way you think. Jenny narrates on her personal struggles of overcoming drug addiction, witchcraft, abandonment, poverty, rejection, abuse, homelessness, and so much more. This book is so riveting and captivating that you will hear the "sound of chains breaking" suddenly off of your life.

The Sound of Freedom speaks directly to perhaps one of the greatest needs in our world today and that is for wholeness, deliverance, healing, love of Christ and the supernatural intervention of God. Here is a book laden with profound encounters with Jesus, angels, visions, life-altering testimonies that offers prophetic declarations, decrees and a practical plan on the road to spiritual recovery and personal victory. The sound of freedom rings and cries out throughout this book and found in the authors' life.

Galatians 5:1 declares *"It is for freedom that Christ has set us free. Stand firm, then, and do not let yourselves be burdened by a yoke of slavery."* Jenny Weaver is a modern-day David with a mandate to carry the sound of deliverance in creating an atmosphere of heaven that brings the glory of God that resounds in her music and ministry. This compact book is fully loaded with the weight of glory that liberates, emancipates and sets in motion ones' total freedom in Christ. I highly recommend this powerful deliverance book for those who have spiritual ears to hear *The Sound of Freedom* ringing!

Dr. Hakeem Collins
Champions International
Author of *Heaven Declares, Prophetic Breakthrough,*
and *Command Your Healing*

I love the teaching of Jenny Weaver's *Sound of Freedom*. This book is for anyone who has a desire to go deeper in the Lord and encounter His glory. Jenny is a spiritual force to be reckoned with when she sings the Scripture and declares God's prophetic promises. This spiritual force is released in the pages of the book. This book is saturated with the spirit of freedom. I highly recommend it to anyone who truly wants to be set free!

MICHELLE MCCLAIN WALTERS
Author, *The Prophetic Advantage* and *Deborah Anointing*

Jenny Weaver is a dynamic force to be reckoned with! I strongly believe that she is one of the hottest upcoming prophetic voices in the worship world today. She is a modern-day Moses and John the Baptist personified in woman form, calling a generation into greater glory and freedom. We have barely begun to see what this vessel of honor is truly carrying! Hear my words when I say that this unique sound is one that will be heard for many generations to come. Ready or not, hear her cry!

Senior Pastor Ben Lim,Th.D.
Ben Lim Ministries
His Way Life
Los Angeles, CA

the Sound of
FREEDOM

the Sound of
FREEDOM

HOW TO BRING THE
GOD OF BREAKTHROUGH
into Your Toughest Struggles

JENNY WEAVER

DESTINY IMAGE® PUBLISHERS, INC.
PO Box 310, Shippensburg, PA 17257-0310
"Promoting Inspired Lives."

This book and all other Destiny Image and Destiny Image Fiction books are available at Christian bookstores and distributors worldwide.

Cover design by Eileen Rockwell
Interior design by Terry Clifton

For more information on foreign distributors, call 717-532-3040.
Or reach us on the Internet: www.destinyimage.com

ISBN 13 TP: 978-0-7684-4997-6
ISBN 13 ebook: 978-0-7684-4998-3
ISBN LP: 978-0-7684-4999-0
ISBN HC: 978-0-7684-5013-2

For Worldwide Distribution, Printed in the U.S.A.
1 2 3 4 5 6 / 22 21 20 19

DEDICATION

This book is dedicated to my dear husband Stephen Weaver.

You have stood by me through so many ups and downs and for 11 years have been the man of my dreams! No one knows me like you do and you truly are my very best friend. Writing this book brought up a lot of old memories and through them all you cheered me on and said "You got this dear." I can't imagine life without you and I want this book to be dedicated to you because without you by my side I don't think I would have made it this far. Love you forever.

CONTENTS

FOREWORD

Jenny Weaver is a fresh voice on the subject of praise and worship. She has a passion and zeal to see true worship in the church. She ministers from a place of revelation and understanding of the importance of worship for every believer. This book is not just for praise and worship leaders, but for all believers.

I want to endorse and recommend this book by Jenny Weaver. I believe this book will give additional insight into one of the most important subjects you can study. I love Jenny Weaver's freedom and this book will free you from the restraint of religion and tradition. The truths in this book will become a part of

your journey to freedom. Through her testimony, Jenny has discovered powerful tools that will empower and encourage you to become everything God has called you to be through the power of worship.

There is a new emphasis on the song of the Lord. The new song will release God's power and grace in your life. It will cause breakthroughs and miracles to be released in your life. Jenny Weaver has seen miracles as she sings the Scriptures and the song of the Lord. This book is an extension of her ministry. It will release miracles and breakthroughs worldwide.

A revelation of worship will change your life. This subject matter is too important to overlook. You should not be ignorant of the power of prophetic worship. Prophetic worship releases the breath of God in the church. Churches that embrace prophetic worship will be full of life and new things.

I pray that the words of this book will challenge and stretch you in the area of worship. God is doing a new thing. He is releasing new wine. He is creating a new wineskin. You cannot have an old wineskin of worship and expect new wine. This book will help prepare a new wineskin. I pray as you read this book that the Lord will give you an understanding of this current move of the Spirit. We are living in exciting times. Worship should be exciting and full of glory and inspiration. Let this book stir you and inspire you to new heights and levels of worship.

JOHN ECKHARDT
Bestselling author, *Prayers That Rout Demons*

CHAPTER 1

A HARSH BEGINNING

From a young age the enemy tried many times to kill me and destroy the plan of God on my life. After facing a few near-death experiences, the grace and mercy and love of God ripped me out of the grips of a demonic hold on my life, turned my entire life around, and now I am a walking, talking, living testimony that God is able to help anyone get free and stay free.

God has a plan for you. God has a good plan for your life no matter what you are walking through right now, or what you've walked through in the past, or what you will go through in the future. Jeremiah 29:11 says, *"For I know the plans I have for you,"*

declares the Lord, "plans to prosper you and not to harm you, plans to give you a hope and a future." Those are words to live by.

The enemy wants to disrupt the plans of God for your life—but he has been defeated and you can walk in absolute and total victory every day of your life. God has come to give you life—abundant life. I went from living a life of absolute turmoil to now living a life more abundantly above all that I could ever ask or even think, because of the saving power of Jesus Christ.

My Testimony

In this book I share the gripping story of my testimony as a drug addict from the streets, to a daughter of the Most High King and living in the rest of God. I include steps, prayers, declarations, and a challenge—providing practical ways for you to have freedom and victory in your own life.

My father is of Jamaican descent; my mother is of Irish descent. They met in Philadelphia, Pennsylvania, and my mother's family was not happy that she was dating interracially. My mother was raised Catholic, but didn't really have a relationship with Jesus Christ. My father was a bad influence on my mom and introduced her to heroin. And they both used heroin for many years.

I was born on January 15, 1982 and am the second oldest of the eight children they had together. And although it should have been a joyous occasion, my mother was addicted to heroin when I was conceived, and she used heroin the entire pregnancy. I was born addicted to drugs and experienced severe withdrawal pain and agony.

My mother tells the story of how she didn't know the Lord at the time as her personal Savior; and as she was withdrawing from heroin as well, she cried out to God in a moment of desperation. She said, "God, if You are real and You can help me, give me a sign." And then she realized a song was playing on the radio by the Carpenters titled "Close to You," with the lyrics, "Why do birds suddenly appear every time you are near?" My mother said she looked out her window and there was a bird sitting on the window ledge, and she knew that was a sign from God—that He was with her. She said at that moment all the withdrawal symptoms left her body and she gave her life to Christ—and has been living for Him ever since.

That was one of the first attempts the enemy tried to take my life. Even before I was born into the world, God had His hand on me the whole time, protecting me. He was protecting me while inside my mother's womb. He has continued to do so all the days of my life.

Filled with the Spirit

I remember at six years of age being filled with the precious Holy Spirit. I was at a revival service with my parents and a guest speaker, a prophet, was conducting the service. Toward the end of the service, he began to call people up to pray for them and prophesy to them. He pointed to me and said, "Young lady, come here, God has a word for you." I didn't move because I didn't think he was talking to me, after all, I was just a child and in my church children weren't called on to be prayed for or given a prophetic word. Yet he called to me again, and immediately I knew it was me he was calling up to the front.

I felt the presence of God all over me and began trembling as I walked down that middle aisle of that old-fashioned Pentecostal church. When I got to the front, he began to prophesy over me and I started to cry. He asked if I wanted to be filled with the Holy Spirit, and I shook my head yes. Then he laid his hands on me and immediately I was filled and fell backward and spoke in tongues for close to 45 minutes. That experience is one I will never forget. The Lord was impacting my life even at such a young age, and I believe it was His divine plan to show me His power at that point of my life.

About one year later, around the age of seven, I had my first encounter of meeting Jesus face to face, and it is to this day one of the most vivid memories I have. I remember it clearly. My sisters and I rode our bikes to the local store in our neighborhood. On our way home, we had to cross a busy intersection, and my older sister told me to wait before crossing. Being obstinate, I didn't want to listen to her. I started pedaling across the road, thinking it was clear of traffic. But when I was in the middle of the road, I looked to my right and saw a car coming straight for me! I heard the screeching of the brakes, but it was too late—the driver didn't have time to stop the car and I watched it hit me head-on.

My bike flew several feet up in the air and came slamming down, twisted and completely destroyed. I was landed face down on the road completely still. My sisters ran over to me, asking if I was okay and crying and screaming. "I'm okay," I told them. The people in the car came over to see if I was alright. The police were called and soon the ambulance arrived. Everyone was very upset and crying. The emergency medical team checked me to make sure I was okay and were in disbelief when they saw I was unharmed—not even a scratch—especially after seeing that my bike was completely demolished.

"I Want to Meet Jesus"

My mother came to take me home since we lived only a few houses away from where I was hit. When she put me to bed that night, I said to her, "Mom, I want to meet Jesus. Is that possible?" She said, "Absolutely, let's pray that you will be able to see Jesus and He will come to you." As I lay there, I went into a dream that was like real life to me. I was suddenly in a beautiful meadow that was covered with white snow, and in front of me was a pathway lined with Christmas-like trees on both sides of the path.

> I REMEMBER FEELING LOVED, AND IT FELT LIKE I WAS HOME.

About a quarter of a mile ahead in the middle of the path, I could see the throne of Jesus and I could see Jesus sitting on the throne. He was motioning for me to come to Him, so I began to walk very carefully down the path and between the trees. As I walked past the trees, they lit up on both sides at the same time with the most beautiful lights. It was the most amazing thing I had ever seen; and as a young child, you can imagine my delight! The trees were lighting up all on their own as I passed by.

I finally reached the place where Jesus was sitting and He put me up on His lap. Just like a loving Father, He began to talk with me, and He put His hand over my heart. I don't recall exactly what He said to me, but I do remember feeling safe. I remember feeling loved, and it felt like I was home.

I was so ecstatic about the dream. To me it wasn't just a dream, it was Jesus actually meeting me and encountering me. From that moment I began to see into the supernatural realm. I began to see angels and demons and even smell foul odors when demons would appear to me. I would shake in such terror. I saw visions of angels flying around and standing in places near me.

This spiritual realm was colliding with the physical realm of my life at home and at school, with my family and my friends.

CHAPTER 2

TOXIC ENVIRONMENTS

My home was a very toxic place to live. My parents were abusive toward each other and also toward me and my brothers and sisters. I remember going to church a lot—it seemed like we went every day for hours at a time. But yet I remember going home after church and being whipped with an extension cord and the metal part of belts and hangers and feeling unloved, feeling unimportant, and thinking that I didn't want anything to do with church if this is how people treated the ones they're supposed to love when they returned home.

My parents were constantly splitting up and getting back together. My dad stumbled back into a drug addiction and would beat up my mom so terribly that her face would be unrecognizable to us. Life was hard as a child growing up with so many siblings and so much turmoil. We were a poor family, and when my dad would leave we had even less income. I remember many nights going without dinner and being so hungry that we would climb over the neighbor's fence to pick their oranges just to have something to eat.

As I entered into my teenage years, schoolwork was very hard and I was made fun of a lot. Specifically, I was called the "ugly sister" by the kids in school. I also started suffering symptoms from vitiligo, an untreatable skin condition where light-colored patches appeared on my skin. I was constantly and severely made fun of for that—something I had no control over. Consequently, I fell into a deep depression during those years.

My father was out of the house most of that time, so my mother was struggling as a single mom with seven children and having to do everything on her own—many times without money or a car. My mind started going into very dark places thinking about ending it all. Around the age of 13, one day after being bullied all day at school, I came home to find my mom very angry and she whipped me for something as silly as not cleaning the kitchen right. So after the beating, I went to my room, closed the door, found a pair of scissors and stared at the scissors for quite a long time. I heard in my spirit, "Cut your wrists. End it all. It's better for everyone if you just go away." And then without hesitation I sliced at my wrist with the scissors until blood began to drip out and in some twisted way I felt at the time that what I did made living better.

Dark Addictions

That day, that act began my addiction of cutting my wrist. When cutting myself, I felt compelled, almost lured, into a darker heaviness that was always over me. And the pain that I would feel was nothing compared to what I was going through emotionally. I began to cut all the time and at one point I had 56 slices on my arm from where I had used razors and scissors to cut myself. My arm was raw and I would have to wear long-sleeved shirts every day—even in the middle of summer in Florida. Every time I would encounter some form of emotional stress, I immediately wanted to relieve it by cutting—and so I did.

There came a point when I realized I needed to stop, but the demonic influence had now such a tight grip on my heart I couldn't stop. I was trapped in a body that I couldn't control anymore. That demonic realm that I opened went deeper when I was introduced to the movie, *The Craft,* which was about four teenage girls who were witches and had incredible power and control to change things around them. My three friends and I watched the movie quite often and we wanted to imitate what we saw, so I was introduced to witchcraft as a young girl and that opened doors that nobody should ever open. For me at the time, the draw to both cutting and witchcraft was the need to control at least a few areas of my life, because in so many other areas—my family, my home life, at school—I felt out of control and helpless to do anything for myself, my siblings, my mother and father.

My home life was even worse now and my dad's cheating and drug use had gotten too much for my mom. My parents divorced and they both remarried very soon after. I hated both my step-mom and my stepdad at first. My stepdad was a recovering addict who quickly fell back into crack cocaine addiction and was also very abusive to my mother—and so the cycle continued. My step-mom ended up being someone I could talk to, so I wanted to be around her. But because she and my dad lived in a small apart-ment, each of my siblings took turns going over his house on the weekends. Being seven of us, it seemed like an eternity until it was my turn again.

In high school I began skipping school and experimenting with pot, marijuana. Music was very influential at that time in my life. I listened a lot to music that talked about drugs and get-ting high and committing suicide. I listened to Kurt Cobain, Janis Joplin, Jimi Hendrix, and Marilyn Manson. The music began to have such a heavy influence on me that I had a deep desire to use drugs and to get high and to cut continuously—try-ing to find love any way I could. In my senior year, I reached out to another student who showed me attention; she was openly gay and seemed confident in who she was. I wanted to be like that. I wanted to be confident and secure in myself.

I began to have feelings for this friend and convinced myself over time that I was just like her. I eventually "came out" as gay and didn't want anything to do with men at all. After all the abuse I had seen and how badly I was made fun of by the boys in school, I thought this would be a better life for me. I would just find a woman who would love me for who I was.

I found that this friend was easy to talk to and that she would listen to me. She would compliment me and tell me that I was pretty. I had not heard that from anyone in my family or anybody I knew up to that point. I hid this relationship with her because I knew that if my family found out, they would consider me to be an embarrassment—it would be a very shameful thing in their minds.

Destructive Lifestyles

The group of friends I was hanging out with accepted the gay lifestyle. Still during my senior year, I began sneaking out of my house at night and stealing my mom's car to go to college parties and adult parties where they were taking the drug ecstasy, drinking alcohol, and smoking pot. I would dress up in revealing clothes and go to the parties. I'd accept drugs and participate in all kinds of activities that I knew deep down I shouldn't have been doing—just to be accepted. My life seemed to be speeding around on a racetrack of trying to be accepted, trying to win approval.

I was trying to deal with heavy rejection and abandonment issues. I had no self-worth, no identity, no idea of the purpose and plan of God for my life at this point, so I didn't care if I was to live or if I was to die at one of those parties. I just wanted to forget everything at home, to forget everything that I wasn't. To forget that I wasn't pretty enough or smart enough according to other people. I wanted all of that to go away. So, I began to drown those thoughts and emotions and feelings in alcohol, ecstasy, and marijuana. I changed my appearance too. I cut my hair so short, like a boy, and I dressed differently. My mom noticed the changes in me and would come into my room and yell at me, telling the demons to come out of me—and then she would punish me.

My grades were slipping, but I didn't care anymore if I would graduate or not. All I cared about was getting high and hanging out with my friends. I remember getting into an argument with my mom over something that I said, and she hit me in the face and my lip began to bleed. I had enough. I couldn't take it anymore at home, so I ran away and moved in with my dad. Once I was at his house I began to sneak out and go to parties again and even got a fake ID to get into clubs.

My mom decided to move away during this time to attend Bible college in Tennessee. My brothers and sisters went with her. Not long after they moved, I got into an argument with my dad and he kicked me out. I had dropped out of high school and had no place to go. I asked all the friends I was partying with if I could stay with them, and I asked the girl who was at this point my girlfriend, and none would let me stay with them. So at 17 years of age I found myself alone, hopeless, and homeless with only a backpack of clothes and the guitar that my father had bought for me years before. I walked the streets until I got so tired I would sleep on the streets.

I would slip under the fence at the local opera house in our downtown area and sleep hiding between two big pillars trying to keep myself safe from other people who lived on the streets and so cops wouldn't find me and take me to a shelter or a teen home.

Torment

Loneliness, fear, torment of the mind, depression, anger, and every terrible feeling filled my heart, my mind, and my spirit.

At a party, I connected with a woman who was almost ten years older, and I began to date her. I was able to stay with her and was, for the time being, off the streets. But in my mind, I was still homeless and alone because I really didn't have any family at that point, and I didn't trust people to care for me and love me. I felt that everyone would turn on me sooner or later, so I never really let anybody in my heart or head.

Then I began to use people to get what I wanted—and at the same time I began to study wicca. I read as many books as I could on wicca and witchcraft. I went to stores that sold stones and spell books and charms and I became a practicing witch.

I later started dating a young man and I had a female roommate who was a witch. Her whole family line of women were witches, and she began to introduce me to another realm of it. We used acid (LSD) and various hallucinogenic drugs to open ourselves more to the spirit world. I would see things move in the house that we lived in and saw images of dark spirits moving around the house, hiding behind doors and such. We lived in fear so much that we believed the house was actually haunted. So, we would perform rituals and incantations and even planted specific flowers to rid the house of the evil that we both knew was there.

Evil Spirits

One evening in the hallway, my roommate and I were discussing seeing a spirit in the house. All of a sudden, the ceiling light above us burst apart with a loud sound and the house went black. Glass shattered all over us and we dropped to the floor trembling and crying in terror. We could literally feel a dark presence all around us.

Other times I would hear a very clear knocking on my bedroom walls when trying to sleep. Fear tormented me severely. Then I began to remember my childhood and the encounters I had with the Lord, and I knew that if I didn't stop practicing witchcraft, I would most likely never come out of it. So I made a decision to not do any more spells out of fear.

Nevertheless, darkness began to cover and control me, and it seemed my life was completely worthless. During this time, I was introduced to heroin and it had one of the strongest grips on my life I'd ever known. I was addicted immediately the first time I tried it. I became so physically addicted to it that I had to have it by my bedside to even be able to get out of the bed to go to the bathroom or to eat or do anything. I once jumped out of a two-story window just to go get high. A boyfriend, who was trying to ween me off of heroin, had locked me in the room, and I risked getting hurt rather than kicking the habit. That part of my life was very dark.

Without the drug I would go through severe withdrawals to the point of my body going into shock and almost dying. The withdrawal effects would last for days with no relief from the physical pain and torment my body was going through, as well as the mental and emotional trauma. After years of being addicted to heroin, I finally decided to get help. I went to a methadone clinic and signed up for treatment so I could be weaned off bit-by-bit—so I could deal with the withdrawal process and still function in my daily life.

After a few months of being on methadone, I finally got off of heroin. I actually started attending church and trying to serve God, but it was short-lived. I soon found myself being lured back into the world. Shame, condemnation, and guilt flooded my mind. I saw myself as a failure constantly. I felt as if I was an embarrassment to my family. I was an adult who had no future, no career, nothing going for me. I was just a drug addict, a loser, and I definitely felt that God was disappointed in me—so much so that He had turned away from me.

The next face of drug addiction was methamphetamine (meth). It was different from heroin because it carried such a heavy, dark demonic presence with it. Meth was felt almost immediately. From the first time I tried it, my mind hallucinated constantly—I saw images and shadows and people who were not there.

Stephen

This was when I was introduced to Stephen, my husband, he was one of the biggest meth dealers in Plant City, about an hour and a half southwest of Orlando, Florida. He was known for taking whatever he wanted and doing whatever he wanted, which included breaking into houses and stealing drugs, taking people's cars, and using violence to come against anyone trying to physically stop him. I remember people being very scared of him; and when they found out he and I were dating, they were scared to even hang out with me for fear of what he might do to them if he found out.

Our relationship was very unstable, toxic, and unhealthy in every way. Most of the time our minds were completely controlled by the drugs, so we were mean to each other and had no regard for the other person at all. But somehow we stayed together. We would talk often about getting off drugs to have a better life. We would share our dreams with each other, and I would tell him about one day getting clean and wanting to lead worship at the church.

Deep down inside me, I knew I was called to sing for the Lord but at this point, that truth was buried under a load of guilt, shame, and chains. I didn't know how to get free. Stephen would share his dreams about wanting to have a nice home and nice family one day. So, we would make plans. Our deal was that one of us had to get off drugs first so that we could help the other one get clean and stay clean. Well, that just so happened to be me.

After two years of being with Stephen and living a fast life as a meth junkie, I got pregnant and had our daughter, Cameron. When I first found out I was going to have a child, I did my best to not use drugs; but that didn't last long. All logic, common sense, and every desire to do good and take care of this new baby went out the window because the addiction was so strong. Getting high completely took over my life and I found myself using even while pregnant—and crying afterward, feeling so guilty. The guilt would make me use drugs even more so that I couldn't feel anything. I would be completely numb to the reality of being pregnant and being a meth addict with no place to go.

CHAPTER 3

FREEDOM SOUNDS LIKE SURRENDER

Sometime in March 2009, I remember very clearly that I had been awake for four or five days in a row and I had not eaten any food. I was on a "meth binge" and I didn't even drink much water. Even through the stupor of the drug, I was getting extremely concerned about my pregnancy, as I was now a few months along.

After a heated argument with Stephen, I ran outside in the middle of the night. It was raining and I fell to my knees, looked up to the sky, and screamed these three words with the loudest

most piercing scream I could muster up, "GOD, HELP ME!" I didn't see a lightning flash or get goose bumps, (two words) but as the tears streamed down my face I knew that God was listening to my surrender to Him. I knew He could see straight through to my heart—and I felt peace at that moment. A peace came over me and I took a deep breath. I just knew something was going to change and God was going to rescue me.

The Road to Recovery

A few days later, I was rescued out of that situation and put in a safe place in a jail recovery program where I was weaned off of meth, given prenatal vitamins, something to eat, a place to rest, and I began treatment toward the road to recovery.

It wasn't an easy road to travel. Although I wasn't using drugs anymore, I had so many harmful strongholds and unhealthy mindsets to deal with in my life. The process to true deliverance did not happen overnight, but the Lord immediately began to show me His hand over my life, His love for me. He taught me who He was and who I was in Him. Revelation after revelation after revelation would hit my spirit and I would be in tears trembling as He wiped away the past, day after day after day.

When I felt my baby kick and move, I was filled with joy knowing that for the remainder of my pregnancy she would be free from drugs. I began to sing over her and talk to her every day. I told her that she was going to be beautiful, smart, a Christian— and that she was going to be healthy. My baby would respond when I spoke to her by moving around inside me and I would laugh, filled with joy and excitement about the new journey we were on together.

During that time I was in a drug treatment facility in a jail. I was a bit nervous because my baby's due date was before my release date—and that scared me. I knew the state would take her from me because I was incarcerated, and I didn't know if I would be able to get her back.

A New Beginning

Thankfully, I met some loving Christian women who would come each day and pray over my belly, that the hand of the Lord would hold Cameron until I was able to be released from jail. I remember the day I was to be released from the program. When my name was called, I was so excited! And at that very moment, I went into labor. I praised God that I was able to have Cameron a few hours after being released on June 30, 2009. She was born completely healthy; and to my surprise, she had the most beautiful bright red hair and green eyes. As I write this book, she is a very vibrant, loving nine-year-old with beautiful blonde curly locks. She loves to sing prophetically and moves in dreams and words of knowledge.

God is so amazing! Through the birth of Cameron my whole life was changed. I call her our miracle baby. Her birth was joyous and I fell in love with her immediately. I was a loving, caring mother, and I vowed to always tell her encouraging things and how to steward her gifts and desires and dreams in life. I'm thankful that the Lord has allowed me to do just that.

Healing Broken Places

After Cameron's birth and my release from the hospital where she was born, I went straight into a rehab facility and stayed there until her first birthday. During that time I went through an agonizing process of letting go of deep, bitter hatred toward almost everyone I came in contact with. I had built up such thick walls to protect myself that it took time to demolish those walls and allow the Lord to heal the broken places—the places of unforgiveness, the places of offense, and the places of bitterness I had harbored since I was a teenager.

I attended classes and learned about how to stay clean. I learned about how to be a good parent. Although those classes were wonderful and I'm thankful I participated in a great program like that, the lessons I learned from the Holy Spirit were more valuable than anything I have ever learned in my entire life. I surrendered myself to Him.

I was released and went back into society to see if I could stay clean, to see if I could still be a good mom, to see if I could have a normal life. I joined a church with Stephen and we began to attend and do our best to be Christians. I now had two little girls, our daughter Cameron and Darian, Stephen's oldest daughter from his first marriage. We finally began to live normal lives and were overjoyed to have our two beautiful girls with us.

I SURRENDERED MYSELF TO HIM.

Darian was in her early teens when she was finally able to move back with her dad. When she was about five years of age, he would leave her with his parents and slowly slipped away into drugs and a life of crime. After a while, she moved in with her grandparents and they pretty much raised her. Now we were all learning how to be a blended family with a lot of past hurts and wounds—and at times it was really hard.

I remember visiting a local church a few times. One day after the service, I walked up to the pastor and his wife and I said, "If you need any help on the worship team, I would love to help out in any way." They were thrilled and said that they had been praying for God to send someone to help. So I joined the worship team. As a brand-new Christian, I didn't know how to really worship God. I didn't lift my hands. I was too scared. I barely sang out loud. I just stood there and sang quietly into the mic and didn't move. That's a huge difference from where I am now.

Communing with God

At home, I would often go into a quiet room in the house when everyone was sleep and play my guitar. I would sing songs to the Lord, and all of a sudden the Lord would enter into that room and encounter me in such a way that I would hear in my spirit the song of the Lord. Then I would sing out that song of the Lord over my life and follow it with singing a response to what He just sang over me. It was a beautiful way of communing with God that I had never heard before. I had never seen or heard anyone sing spontaneous or prophetical songs, so I began to research the topic on the internet to see if anyone else was doing this. To my surprise, I found many people were singing the prophetic songs of the Lord and spontaneous songs as well.

And so I began to do my own study and ask questions such as what is prophetic worship, because those terms were completely unfamiliar to me. I would read in the Bible Scriptures about the glory of God and Moses, the Ark of the Covenant, the Tabernacle and David, and in the book of Revelation I read about the worship that goes on around the throne constantly. I would be glued to my Bible and had books surrounding me on all sides, and my journals were open, ready for me to record my findings. In the background I would have worship music playing. I was experiencing a whole different world—and my hunger grew more and more every day for God.

Deliverance—a Beautiful Sight

Although I had asked the Lord into my heart, I still had to go through deliverance and I can tell you it was a beautiful sight. I was invited to a deliverance service at a local church in my town. I was happy to go because I was curious about deliverance. At the end of the teaching, the speaker said, "We're now going to pray for individuals who feel like they want extra prayer."

A lady came over to me and wanted to pray with me. I said sure, because I knew in my heart I was saved, that I loved the Lord and there was absolutely no way that I had any demons in me, on me, surrounding me, or however people want to put it nowadays. So she began to pray and looked me right in the eyes and said, "I see you in there, come out right now in the name of

Jesus!" You can imagine my surprise when she said that. I was thinking, *This woman has lost her mind. There are absolutely no evil spirits in me—I'm a Christian.*

She went on like that for a few minutes and I stood there uncomfortable and awkward wanting it to be over so I could go home and go to bed. But then all of a sudden, as she placed her Bible on top of my head and said again, "I command you, evil spirit, come out of her!" it was like I was now sitting outside myself watching what was going on—like a movie in front of me. I could hear and see everything, but it was no longer me who was in charge. Evil spirits began to growl and scream and scratch my body with my own fingernails, trying to open the same scars that I had on my wrist from when I was a teenager and cut myself.

A member of the deliverance team asked two men to come over and hold my arms down because I tried to physically attack the woman who was praying over me. She asked the spirits, "What is your name?"

One said, "Witchcraft."

She asked, "How did you get in there?"

"She opened the door when she looked up spells on the internet as a teenager."

After that, the woman and a man spoke the name of Jesus over and over to cast out the demons. After about an hour or so, I was free, free indeed. Jesus set me free—and only by His name do I testify today that I am absolutely delivered—because He loves me so much.

True Passion and Zeal

My worship began to change after that moment. I was no longer bound by fear; now I was no longer held down by strongholds. I began to worship freely, full of energy and excitement, true passion and zeal for the Lord. Week after week my heavenly Father would show me more about true worship in spirit and truth, more about who He is and who I am in Him—and that truth began to thrust me into my true calling as a worshipper and His daughter.

I became a worship leader for a local church and I call that season of my life a "spiritual training camp," as I had the most amazing encounters with the Lord—but also the most intense warfare and spiritual attacks I had ever gone through. I would have tremendous highs on the mountaintop with the Lord. Then it seemed like only moments later I was hit with everything but the kitchen sink from people who came against me with vicious words. I experienced feelings of frustration and wanting to give up and never sing again, never step foot in a church again.

A few days later, the Lord would wrap me up again in His arms and give me the strength to keep going. This seesaw of ups and downs continued for a few years. Now, I'm so thankful for those moments because I realize that the Lord was teaching me and training me to reach out to the nations.

CHAPTER 4

FREEDOM SOUNDS
LIKE RESTORATION

In this process of purifying and refining me, I went through a beautiful transformation and time of restoration. In my early 20s, my father and stepmom were sentenced to prison for drugs and a whole list of crimes. My stepmother was sentenced to 17 years in prison and my father received a life sentence in prison. When I was told the news, I was too high to give it a second thought. Years and years went by and my heart had grown hard toward him; there was such bitterness for him not being there for us as a dad and a good father figure.

I was really angry that my brothers didn't have a dad to teach them and train them up right. We had our mom and she did the best she could at the time. Whenever anyone would mention my dad to me, I'd say, "I don't have a dad, but if I did and he passed away, then God bless his soul but I won't shed even one tear." Well one day in October 2016, as I was teaching my daughter a homeschool lesson, I received a call from my older sister. This was strange because even though my siblings and I all love each other, we rarely call to chat. We don't have that kind of relationship. So when I saw her number come up on the phone, I answered right away.

She proceeded to tell me that our dad was released from his life sentence and was now in the hospital on life support in Florida. The hospital was investigating to find family members who could make the decision to keep him on life support or take him off. Because she was in another state, she asked me if I would. My heart began to beat so fast. Thoughts flooded my heart and mind, *I don't know this man. It's not my responsibility. If it's his time to go, then let him just go.* So I told her to ask another one of our siblings, and I ended the call and went back to teaching Cameron.

A few minutes later, I felt a tug on my heart from the Holy Spirit. I kind of shook it off because I wasn't ready to go to that hospital and see my dad after 17 years of no contact with him. Another tug and then another came until I finally got up and went to talk to my husband who happened to be off work that day. When I told Stephen about the call, he said, "I feel you need to go. I'll go with you." I began to panic at the thought of seeing my father, but after a long talk, my husband convinced me to just go and sign the papers at least and pray with him.

I said, "I'll go, but I'm not talking to him at all. I don't know him and he doesn't know me!" Stephen, Cameron, and I headed to the hospital, which was a little over an hour's drive away. Man, it seemed as if we were never going to arrive. After we parked and entered the hospital, we approached the room and my husband walked right in, but I stood in the hallway frozen with fear.

Frozen Versus Melted

I refused for at least five or ten minutes to go into the room. I stared at his feet at the edge of the bed as that was all I could see from where I stood frozen. Childhood memories flooded my mind. Finally, I took a step toward the door, but stopped. My husband called to me to come in, nodding that everything was okay. I took another step and another, until I walked into the room and saw my dad's face; it was like passing through that doorway melted off 17 years of bitterness, unforgiveness, anger, rejection, and a whole bunch of other strongholds that had gripped me for years and held me hostage.

I walked right up to him—he looked so skinny and frail. He used to be a tall, strong, bulky guy who carried himself with a proud stride. But this man I was looking at was about 135 pounds and had sunken cheeks. There were machines all around him with tubes here and there to keep him breathing and alive. My heart was instantly filled with love. I can't really explain what happened that day, but I know it was only through the Holy Spirit that my heart was so tender toward him.

I sat right by him and held his hand. With tears I said, "Dad, I'm here. It's your daughter Jennifer. Everything's gonna be okay." And I began to pray and pray, and hours went by and then we were told that it was time for visitors to leave. He never moved an inch or blinked an eye, but I talked with him like he was wide awake. I introduced to him to Cameron, whom he had never seen, and my husband, too. I told him, "I will come back and see you, Dad. I love you." And we left.

The next morning, I opened my eyes and immediately jumped out of bed to go see my dad. I wasn't sure if he was worse or better, but I had my dad back in my life and I wanted to love on him before he left this world. I drove to the hospital with Cameron and we were told that he was in the same condition. A doctor pulled me aside and told me it would be best if I just let him go in peace, to take him off the machines. But in my spirit I felt he would live. So I said that, and they looked at me like I was crazy. My dad had heart failure, 13 stints, COPD, his brain was turning into mush, his kidneys were failing, and he was in a coma. It looked hopeless, but I heard from God and I believed, so I stayed by his bed reading him the Bible and singing and praying over him for about eight hours until visiting hours were over. I drove home. The next day I did that same over-an-hour drive back to the hospital. But on that third day, as I turned the corner in the hospital hallway and walked into the room, I saw my dad lying there with his eyes wide open watching television. I was shocked!

"Oh my God, you're awake!"

He could barely talk, but he whispered, "Hi." I walked over to where he could see me and said, "Do you know who I am?" He shook his head yes and I asked, "Who am I?" In his scratchy whisper, he responded, "You're my daughter, Jennifer." My eyes filled with tears. We were reunited after all those years.

I introduced him to Cameron, and he reached up and touched one of her curls and said, "Wow." I called my husband and put him on speaker to say hello to my dad. But Dad would go in and out of sleep so much it was hard to get him to say much. I was just happy God was turning around our relationship. After another two weeks in the hospital, he was to be released to a nursing home. For the next three or so months, I drove to see him almost every other day and would sit by him for hours at a time just reading the Bible and loving him the best I could.

"You're Beautiful"

He said three important things to me in those three months he was with me. He woke up once and called me close. I had to put my ear right up to his face to hear what he was saying, and I heard clearly the third time he repeated it, "Have I ever told you that you're beautiful?" I said, "Hmmm, I don't recall if you have." He said, "You are. You're beautiful." I smiled and said, "Thank you, Dad."

There was another time when my dad just blurted out, "I'm proud of you," and that made me smile too because Dad had never before spoken those words to me, not in my whole life. He told me, as he slipped in and out of consciousness, that he loved me, and I always responded saying, "I love you too, Dad, and I'm here for you."

Those three months meant so much to me because I finally had my dad back and I was so happy to be his caregiver so he wouldn't have to die alone. Some of my siblings weren't able to come visit him, and I wanted him to know he had me by his side, no matter what. Others in our family were still bitter toward him and it broke my heart, especially because they were believers. Wheresin abounds grace should abound even more, but they couldn't let go of the past and forgive. Forgiveness is a key to lasting breakthrough, which I will discuss in more detail later. Dad passed away with my family around him, and he was ready to go home to the Lord.

Restored for Purpose

Right after the root of rejection began to be destroyed in my life, one night while worshipping in my secret place at home, the Lord began to reveal to me the true purpose of reuniting me with my dad. God told me that He wanted to show me in the natural what is taking place in the supernatural between Him and me. He was teaching me about who He really is and who I am in Him. He wanted me to know that all those positive statements that my dad spoke to me are the same as what God has been whispering to me all the while.

My heart felt like it was bursting into a million pieces. Tears began to flow and for hours I sat on the floor and cried out to God; I heard Him speaking to my heart and restoring years and years of walking in darkness. There were many nights like that, nights when He encountered me and my life was radically changed each and every time. The most amazing encounter is when I was taken into the heavens.

It was the third day of a fast to which I had committed myself. That night I heard the Holy Spirit tell me to go get supplies so I could take Communion. I went out of my prayer room and got a cracker and some juice and returned to my prayer room where I had already been praying and worshipping for a few hours that night. I was shown right where I should read in the Bible and I blessed the "bread and the cup" and took Communion (see 1 Corinthians 11:24-25). All of a sudden a heavy presence of the Lord came into the room as I was face down on my wood floor on a mat I used for prayer. The presence of God was so thick I didn't even want to lift my head or move in any way.

As I lay there, I said in my heart, *Father, I want to see You tonight.* All of a sudden, twin angels came down and they both spoke at the same time saying the same thing. One was on my left side and the other was on my right side. I was taken aback by hearing and seeing them! In an instant, they grabbed my arms and we shot up into the heavens going faster than anything I could ever imagine. Once we arrived, one angel took me to a huge field that had a bluish tint to it. I'm not even sure why the color stuck in my mind, but that's how I remember it. Sitting in this field were thousands of people playing guitars. Some of the guitars were unique, very early versions of the instrument, and some were newer models—each one was different.

DIFFERENT TUNES, ONE PERFECT MELODY.

The angel put me in this field and said, "This is where you will play when you come here." All of sudden I saw a beautiful, white open pavilion with four posts holding it up, and the Lord was sitting there in the middle listening to all of us play. Although we all were playing different tunes, the sound was made into one perfect melody.

I was shown around by this angel, and the best part was when the angel took me to see Jesus face to face. I looked up into one part of heaven, and there was Jesus. He did the most amazing thing. When He saw me, He bent down like a parent would and motioned for me to come to Him. I could see He had the most loving smile and He was overjoyed to see me. I took off running and when I got to Him, I embraced Him tightly.

I always thought that when I met Jesus I would tell Him, "Thank You" and "I love You," or tell Him how great He is. But in that moment of actually seeing Him, I could only say three words over and over and over as I was hugging Him, "You're so beautiful, You're so beautiful, You're so beautiful!" Words cannot describe Him—His beauty and glory are phenomenal.

Why did the Lord take me to the heavens? It wasn't so I could have an amazing story or sound spiritual, it was so He could be known even more by His people and He could be lifted high. Since that encounter, my worship has been at such a deep level. I can never in all my life unsee what I saw that day.

Grace and Mercy

In the summer of 2017, my husband and I got pregnant and we were super excited. We posted our unique baby-reveal pictures on social media and had thousands of people rejoicing with us. I remember going for my first check-up and the nurse had a funny look on her face. She told me that I must have given the wrong dates because she could not see the baby just yet. She only saw a tiny speck.

So I just thought that somehow I calculated wrong and forgot about it until my second sonogram. I was told that something was going on because they couldn't find the baby, but I was still showing that I was pregnant. After a bunch of tests and after about three days of praying and seeking God and having all my family and my pastor praying for us, I started experiencing terrible pains. My husband took me to the emergency room, and shortly afterward we were told that we lost the baby. We were not expecting that report at all and we burst into tears. I began screaming, "No! No!"

But before we left the hospital, a peace came over us. I can't really explain it, because in that moment of great loss, most people wouldn't think there would be any peace or even a smile, but we were able to smile and feel His peace because our sovereign God is full of grace and mercy. He surrounded us with His love and in that moment we both made up in our minds that our God was still good. And even though we didn't understand why it happened like that, we were not going to turn our backs on God. We were not going to blame Him, and we were not going to go backward in our walk with the Lord or in our ministry. We were going to hold fast to His word and His faithfullness and His goodness all the days of our life.

> A MIND THAT BELIEVES GOD
> IS A GOOD GOD, IS A MIND
> THAT CANNOT BE SHAKEN.

And let me tell you, my friend, that kind of strength only comes from our heavenly Father. He's the only One who can bring you to that point in your mind when something devastating occurs. That all happened on a Wednesday night, and that Sunday morning I stood on the platform with my guitar and I sang out with a loud voice praising unto our God. The atmosphere began to shift and the glory of God was ushered into the room—the sacrifice of praise made the way for the King of glory.

A mind that believes God is a good God, is a mind that cannot be shaken. We can stand on the foundational truth that no matter what we go through, His mercy truly does endure forever and ever. Amen.

CHAPTER 5

LIFE LESSONS ON THE ROAD TO FREEDOM

I have often wondered why people are so interested in my testimony, then it hit me—they want hope, they want to believe. In the world we live in, people want to hear about and know that miracles still exist. They want to believe that if God will set one person free from pain and turmoil, then surely He will set them or their loved ones free too. They want to be able to hope that they can live an abundant life.

I want to share with you the key lessons I have learned while journeying through life.

Who You Really Are

You can't go anywhere or do anything in life if you have no clue who you really are! So many believers actually struggle in this area and it's the area the enemy fights hard to keep believers from handling. He prevents you from knowing who you really are because he knows if you know the truth then that very truth will set you free—and whom the Son sets free is free indeed! (See John 8:36.)

So where do we start figuring out who we really are? We start by knowing who *God* really is. I know, I know, you probably just thought, *Well, I know who He is—He's God and He's the Creator and He's my Savior.* And all of that is good, but I mean we need to really take time to get to know the personality of God, what He's like, what He's thinking or saying at any given moment, and to know how He responds. We need to go deeper, not just believe what we may have been told or taught, but to really know God in such a way that we could never ever be shaken about who He is.

Getting to know my husband and his character and ways didn't just fall into my lap the moment my friend told me who he was and described him to me. I had to invest time in getting to know him, and eventually I was sure of who he was. If someone was to come to me today and say, "Stephen did this or that...," and it doesn't line up with what I know about him, I don't receive it as fact. I would respond, "No way, that's not my husband, he would never do that." If someone comes to me laughing and tells me something silly my husband did, after hearing it I could easily say without hesitation, "Yep, that's him!" After almost 12 years, I *know* him and I can't be swayed to believe lies about him.

YOU MUST KNOW HIS VOICE JUST LIKE YOU KNOW YOUR OWN.

This is how you are to know God. You must seek Him for yourself. Your pastor can't be in the middle of your relationship with the Lord! I believe in having pastors and mentors and apostles and spiritual fathers and mothers, but *you* must know *His voice* just like you know your own. That will only come through time spent with Him and training your spiritual ear and spirit to be sensitive to how He moves and how He communicates with you.

The beautiful thing is, the journey of knowing Him on this earth is never going to stop! He takes us from glory to glory. Just when you think you've figured Him out, He shows another side to His majesty and beauty. That's why David says in Psalm 27:4 (NKJV), *"One thing I have desired of the Lord, that will I seek: That I may dwell in the house of the Lord all the days of my life, to behold the beauty of the Lord...."* He's saying, God, I just want to look at You and see all there is to see about You.

Knowing Truth Sets You Free

To know God is the beginning of knowing who you are. People the world over are searching for answers to why they are here, who they are, and what is their purpose—but without first knowing God our Father, their pursuit is an endless maze leading to nothing.

Ask yourself this, *Do I really **really** know who God, Jesus, and the Holy Spirit are?* This is basic truth and we must lay this foundation, then build upon it.

In the beginning God—stop right there! Here we have it, the story of how everything begins and ends with God. He is the uncreated One. He always was, He is, and He always will be. The Bible says He is the everlasting Father. Let's take a look into His Word.

John 1:1 (NJKV) says, *"In the beginning was the Word, and the Word was with God, and the Word was God."* This verse is talking about Jesus being the Word and being with God and being God! I love how John 1:14 says, *"The Word became flesh and made [Jesus] dwelling among us. We have seen his glory, the glory of the one and only Son, who came from the Father, full of grace and truth."* John 4:24 says, *"God is spirit"*—again, stop right there. His Holy Spirit is the third member of this beautiful Trinity. He is the One who is with us here on earth, both the Father and the Son are in heaven. He is not vapor, He is a person.

What actually makes a person? The person's spirit, not the body. The Holy Spirit is the Spirit of Jesus and the Spirit of God. He is so precious that the Father and the Son both protect Their Spirit. The Bible says not to grieve the Holy Spirit, it doesn't say not to grieve Jesus or Father God, but specifically the Holy Spirit. Jesus Himself declares in Mark 3:29: *"but whoever blasphemes against the Holy Spirit will never be forgiven; they are guilty of an eternal sin."* Wow, that says a lot about how the Father and the Son view and hold the Holy Spirit in such high regard.

Too many view the Holy Spirit as the lesser of the Trinity, but that's not the case. If you want to go deeper as a believer and worshipper, you must understand this foundational truth. There is no competition or discord in the Trinity. They each know their identity, their function, their place, and they know they are perfect. They are all three in one and are God. Begin to communicate with the Holy Spirit just like you would talk to Jesus, and thank Him for being your Comforter, Advocate, Helper. You will find that by acknowledging the precious Spirit of God, the doors of the supernatural will open up to you like you couldn't imagine.

The Original Plan

The Father's original plan was to give us a beautiful life with His Spirit, to fellowship with us daily, to give us an assignment, and to be fruitful and multiply. That's exactly what we see happening in the beginning with God creating the world and making Adam and Eve.

Adam and Eve didn't lack for anything and came to God unashamed and without fear every day to walk with Him. They knew Him so well, the Bible says in Genesis 3:8, that they heard the sound of the Lord walking. Wow, they were so sensitive and knew God so well that they could tell when He was walking in the Garden. They noticed it was Him. God gave them authority and dominion and set up parameters and structure to protect them. He even let them tend the garden He created and placed them in.

God has not strayed from what He wanted then and what He intends for us. He still is looking for those who will walk with Him, know His voice, follow after Him, and follow His commandments from a place of love and relationship. He still wants His sons and daughters to be fruitful and multiply (see Genesis 1:22). That doesn't mean just having children, it means to prosper even as your soul prospers, to have life and have it more abundantly (see Genesis 9:7). He still wants us to walk in the authority and dominion He bestowed on His creation back in the beginning. He is the same yesterday, today, and forever (see Hebrews 13:8). God wants His family. We are part of the family He desires. You are part of the family He desires, loves, and wants to be with Him for eternity.

> GOD IS ABSOLUTELY GOOD, REGARDLESS OF OUR EARTHLY CIRCUMSTANCES.

So many people, even believers, measure who God is by their own life experiences and that is a trick of the enemy, just like in the Garden when he tried to discount God's Word to Eve. People think if someone dies, a marriage doesn't work out, or a family member is suffering, that God is the one who caused it or allowed it. Listen to me, we must go only by what the Word of God says God is, not our circumstances. He is absolutely amazing, and He is absolutely good, regardless of earthly circumstances.

God Is Good

God is always being blamed for a lot of things that He just isn't doing. We can put to rest wondering if it is His will to heal us, it *is* His will! That's exactly why Jesus took the stripes on His back. The Bible doesn't just confirm it once in the Old Testament, but again in the New Testament—see Isaiah 53:5 and First Peter 2:24. Jesus willingly suffered for us; He was whipped, His back brutally struck again and again—for our healing.

Let's also put to rest any thought that God is up in heaven making people sick or causing them to be in terrible situations so He can "get their attention." Those are traits of evil parents. Our good Father would not do that to His children—to us. I want you to resolve in your mind the truth that God, Jesus, and the Holy Spirit are purely good in nature and loving parents!

Study the nature of God, study His character, read about the life of Jesus again, this time with the intent to know His character and His personality and His truth! This is a step people don't understand when it comes to walking in lasting breakthrough and walking in their true identity. So many people want an instant change, like the microwave generation we're in today. They attend a conference or service to get someone to pray over their situation, but that isn't all there is to it. Each believer must personally strive to renew his or her entire mind by His Word. I ask God to give me a hunger for His Word and a deep desire to study His Scriptures and to actually understand what He is saying for that particular moment or situation in my life.

Mind Renewal Homework

If at all possible today or this week, set aside time to read, study, and understand one of the four Gospels (Matthew, Mark, Luke, or John) of your choice. Write in a journal, type notes on your computer, or record into your smartphone what you hear God speaking to you through your study of His Word.

After I had demons cast out of me, I didn't automatically understand my true identity or purpose in Christ and start immediately walking in lasting breakthrough. My deliverance was a part of a beautiful process that is ongoing. Daily I'm being changed. Yes, I'm free and free indeed, and I'm going from glory to glory as well (see 2 Corinthians 3:18 NKJV). And I thank Him for each step I take. There are levels to this Christian walk!

Write out the attributes of God you discover in the Gospel and meditate on His goodness and His mercy. For example, God is good, faithful, merciful, all-knowing, all-powerful, everywhere, a gentleman, loving, holy.

Write out things God certainly is *not:* evil, a thief, a murderer, deaf, limited in power.

Take time to think about and record simple exercises such as establishing and reaffirming the truth of who He is and who He isn't. This is the foundation of your faith as a believer, your mindset, your spiritual worldview of life, your road to freedom and eternal life.

Prayer

My heavenly Father, I want to truly know You! I don't want to have just knowledge about You from others or even from what I read. I want to encounter You and experience You like I never have before. Forgive me if I thought You were doing things in my life that You weren't. I'm ready and open now to the truth from Your Holy Spirit. Holy Spirit, reveal Jesus to me more and more. Transform my mind every day and make me more like Him. Lord, I love You and I want a deep desire and hunger to study the Word and seek You in all my ways. I love You, my Father, in Jesus' name, amen.

Declarations

When you declare, you are making a statement that you firmly believe and will live by. I offer the following declarations for you to absorb into your life—your more-than-abundant, victorious life.

I DECLARE in my life that God is good and every good gift comes from Him (James 1:17).

I DECLARE in my life that God is my Healer and my Provider (Isaiah 53:5; 1 Peter 2:24; Matthew 6:25-34).

I DECLARE in my life that God's will for me is to prosper and succeed (Jeremiah 29:11).

I DECLARE in my life that God is merciful and loving (Exodus 34:6; Jonah 4:2).

I DECLARE in my life that God is for me, not against me and my family (Psalm 56:9).

I DECLARE in my life that God is all-powerful and able (Matthew 19:26).

I DECLARE in my life that God is faithful to fulfill His promises (2 Corinthians 1:20).

I DECLARE in my life that God is leading me into all truth (Deuteronomy 32:4; Psalm 31:5; 2 John 1:3).

I DECLARE in my life that God is my Protector and Deliverer (Genesis 14:20; Psalm 18:2; Galatians 1:4).

I DECLARE in my life that I know God more and more each day (Exodus 6:7; Numbers 24:16; Deuteronomy 4:35; Judges 18:5; Psalm 46:10).

CHAPTER 6

WHO AM I?

Who am I? This is one of my favorite subjects because so many people have no idea who they are actually called to be. They believe they are here on earth only to *serve* God. Yes, we love to serve the Lord, but we are also sons and daughters of God; and from that perspective, serving is really just loving Him, it's not a job or chore. A servant or orphan who is made to serve behaves and thinks different from a true child of a loving parent.

The Bible says *"in love [God] predestined us for adoption to sonship through Jesus Christ..."* (Eph. 1:5). Did you catch that? God predetermined and already planned for us to be His children

through the life and resurrection of His Son, Jesus. Before you were even a thought by your parents, God saw you and knew you and planned to adopt you as His very own. That is who you are; you are not a mistake or forgotten—extensive plans and measures were taken to make sure you would have a way to your loving, heavenly Father to become His child.

One of my favorite verses is Romans 8:14-16:

> For **those who are led by the Spirit of God are the children of God**. The Spirit you received does not make you slaves, so that you live in fear again; rather, the Spirit you received brought about your adoption to sonship. ... The Spirit himself testifies with our spirit that we are God's children.

Let me make this truth super easy to understand. My daughter, Cameron, is one of my greatest joys in life. Her father and I truly adore her; she is such an amazing daughter to us, so naturally we love her dearly. Cameron is confident in her identity as our daughter; she doesn't question if she is or is not. If she makes a mistake, she doesn't hang her head low and wonder if we want her around anymore. She doesn't think that all of a sudden she stopped being our child. It may even sound silly when we think of it like that, but many believers worldwide often have these thoughts when they think about their walk with the Lord. They wonder if they measure up to being His child through their actions. If they make a mistake or slip up, they automatically think that God has turned His back on them and is disappointed in them.

From the Beginning

Let's go all the way back to the beginning to see exactly how God responded in the Garden of Eden when Adam and Eve ate from the tree that God said not to. After their disobedience, they hid from God. Notice that God did not hide from them. God came to the Garden, like He did every day, to fellowship and be with His kids. But they didn't come out to meet Him like usual. Because God is omniscient, we know He already knew what happened, yet we see He still came to meet with them. He called out, "Adam, where are you?" He continued to talk with them even though He knew they disobeyed Him. After it was all said and done, God even made them clothes and covered them. From the beginning, God was and still is good, loving, faithful, and forgiving.

If this is how God responded then, why do so many people think that when they mess up it pushes God away from them and He can't stand the sight of sin and such. God hates sin because it causes His children to run and hide from Him—not the other way around. He sought them out and covered them and even revealed His plan to redeem what was lost there in the Garden. What was lost? Their relationship with God, their daily fellowship with Him.

Most people don't run straight to Father God when they miss the mark because of their own shame and condemnation. And on top of that, the enemy loves to keep reminding us of our failures and tries to distort the character of God and His tender heart toward us.

JESUS IS THE ANSWER
TO EVERY PROBLEM.

For an abundant life of freedom, God's sons and daughters must live their Christian lives focused on Jesus as the answer to problems. They are marked with a life of victory, healings—and signs and wonders follow them because they truly believe. They don't struggle through life. They go through trials like everyone else, but they stand on His Word and know He is with them. They aren't trying to get out of this earthly life and just focus on getting to heaven one day. They understand that the Kingdom of God is also within them; and although they are looking for His appearing, they are able to see Him and walk with Him through communion with His Holy Spirit every day! They rest in His goodness.

Those with an orphan mentality live their Christian lives focused on their problems and seem to have a longer *prayer* list than a *breakthrough and victory* list. Difficult situations can too easily move them from a place of faith and trust in God to worry and despair. When bad news comes their way, in one voice they say they trust and have faith, yet in another they frantically stress out. They get saved but struggle through this life, just getting by while they wait to get to heaven one day. They have a "me first" mentality and worry about how something affects them, how it benefits them, and what they can get out if it. They never live in the fullness and favor of God the way He intended.

If that describes your Christian life up to this point, there's hope for you, my friend! It's not by accident that you are reading this book—the Holy Spirit has been leading your steps and wants to reveal truth to your spirit so you can live in absolute and complete freedom.

Know who you are! Walk in it!

I encourage you to read and meditate on the following Scriptures from God's Word:

> *For those who are led by the Spirit of God are the children of God. The Spirit you received does not make you slaves, so that you live in fear again; rather, the Spirit you received brought about your adoption to sonship. And by him we cry, "Abba, Father"* (Romans 8:14-15).

> *So in Christ Jesus you are all children of God through faith* (Galatians 3:26).

> *See what great love the Father has lavished on us, that we should be called children of God! And that is what we are! The reason the world does not know us is that it did not know him. Dear friends, now we are children of God, and what we will be has not yet been made known. But we know that when Christ appears, we shall be like him, for we shall see him as he is* (1 John 3:1-2).

> *The Spirit himself testifies with our spirit that we are God's children. Now if we are children, then we are heirs—heirs of God and co-heirs with Christ, if indeed we share in his sufferings in order that we may also share in his glory* (Romans 8:16-17).

Those aren't just any old Scriptures, those are essential keys to realizing and accepting the truth of who you are in Christ so it can take root and really begin to transform your life. Read these passages from the Bible a few times and watch them transform your thinking. The only way to break out of wrong thinking is to receive truth and to know it so it can set you free.

Prayer

My Father, I thank You for revealing to my heart the truth about who I really am in You. Today I shake off my old thinking of how I used to see myself and I put on the new nature of the Spirit of Life and take my place as Your very own child. I ask that You keep guiding me in all truth, and I pray Your peace will guard my heart as I step into my destiny and calling, in Jesus' mighty name. Amen.

Declarations

I DECLARE in my life I have the mind of Christ (1 Corinthians 2:16).

I DECLARE in my life that I'm God's beloved child (John 1:12).

I DECLARE in my life that I've been bought with a price (1 Corinthians 6:20; 7:23).

I DECLARE in my life that all shame and condemnation is gone from my heart now (Romans 8:1).

I DECLARE in my life that I lack for nothing because my Father supplies all my needs (James 1:4; 1 Timothy 6:17).

I DECLARE in my life that I am divinely chosen by God for such a time as this (Esther 4:14).

I DECLARE in my life that I'm not a mistake, forgotten, or overlooked by God (Deuteronomy 31:6; Joshua 1:5; Hebrews 13:5).

I DECLARE in my life that I'm the head and not the tail (Deuteronomy 28:13,44).

I DECLARE in my life I'm above and beyond a conqueror through Christ (Romans 8:37).

I DECLARE in my life that my God is for me and never against me (Psalm 42:4; Romans 8:31).

CHAPTER 7

BREAKTHROUGH

My life is one that speaks loudly of a real breakthrough. I broke away from the dark and lonely streets of addiction and abuse to now enjoying a place in God that is overflowing with His presence and blessing. It takes my breath away at times when I sit to reflect on His goodness and remember where I came from.

So many people today that I meet are searching for a breakthrough in their lives—whether in their marriage, with their kids, for various addictions, their thinking, or in their spiritual growth. Some want breakthrough in their finances, for the poverty cycle to be broken. There are so many other strongholds that people want to break through and conquer.

So the questions on the hearts and minds of those who are being held back are, "How do I get my breakthrough?" and "What are the steps I have to take in order to really see a change for the better in my life?" I'm going to share with you what has worked for me in my life and what I've learned over the past ten years of my new life in Christ.

Surrender

Surrender is first. Surrendering may sound easy, I know, but many people have become so used to their current situation, even though it's not a good one, that it's hard to truly surrender that area and give it up for something better—freedom. In a family, a praying mother may have been overprotective, always coming to the rescue of a child on drugs or living in the world. She will be reluctant to take her hands off the situation and surrender it to God. She will be hard-pressed to really put it all on God to change the circumstance—but only He can bring lasting change.

The same with an addiction that feels as if it has become part of your personality. Surrendering all that is preventing you from being the person God created you to be is essential for you to experience any kind of freedom. And the freedom your heavenly Father offers you is priceless and can flood your life today—right now you can know peace.

Surrender your addiction, unhealthy relationships, eating disorders, whatever it is. Surrender it to God even if you don't feel like you're ready to let go. In prayer, let God know your heart that you're not sure exactly how to surrender it all but you are coming to Him for help because your heart wants breakthrough and you know it's only found in Christ.

Surrendering may sometimes be a daily conversation with the Lord. I did that with cigarettes when I wanted to give them up but I didn't let them go right away. I told God I wanted to be tobacco-free, but I needed help in the area of true surrender. I had to confess my freedom and trust that strength was coming from the Lord. I'm happy to say He delivered me and the desire is not there; in fact, the smell at times has made me sick in my stomach. He will give you all new desires and erase even the trace of what used to be. That's what the transforming blood of Jesus can do!

Surrender is one of the first things Jesus mentioned when He said, "If anyone desires to come after Me, let him deny himself..." (see Matthew 16:24 NKJV). This step is the way to true breakthrough!

JESUS IS THE BREAKTHROUGH!

I've heard countless people say that for believers to experience a breakthrough, they should sow this much, turn around three times and jump up and down, turn to their neighbor and yell "Breakthrough!" and their breakthrough will come. My friend, that's not biblically sound truth or advice. Many people travel so far to conference after conference and event to event desperate for breakthrough. Although I believe in being with like-minded believers to stir your faith and experience fellowship, you must know this truth—Jesus is the breakthrough. Your surrender invites Him into that area to do what only He can do. Yes, go get your faith stirred, but when you're home on that next Monday morning, your life laid down before Him, that is when you will see the miracle unfold.

When you surrender that particular area or your entire life over to Jesus, He takes you and lovingly places you where you need to be. His plans for you are not to harm you but to give you a hope and a future. He then tells you what next steps to take and what direction to move in. He directs your path and doesn't leave you or forsake you—He makes that used-to-be crooked path straight! The road to breakthrough is walking with Jesus down the surrendered path with your hands up, white flag waving, and your life laid down at His feet.

Do that now if you haven't already. Say the following prayer and add to it your own words and your own heart—surrendering whatever you need to for a breakthrough.

Prayer

Father God, I come to You now and I willing lay down (say the thing you need breakthrough for) _____ . I know that only You have the power to bring the changes needed in this area of my life, and today I put it at Your feet. I confess that if I've tried to do it my way, that I now completely surrender and hold nothing back. Please do whatever You need to do, Holy Spirit, and I ask You to give me the strength and grace to trust Your plans—no

> *matter what. Your Word is true and You will move on my behalf and direct my path as I trust in You and acknowledge You in all my ways. In the mighty name of Jesus, I pray. Amen.*

Release Your Sound

The enemy was after my voice from even before I was born! He knows that a believer, a true son or daughter of God, who knows who they are and are completely free is the most dangerous weapon in the world!

Freedom has a sound! I was being set free in my secret place behind closed doors by lifting up my true, original sound to God, unashamed uninhibited, getting on my face and being free in His presence. Day after day I was being transformed right before my very eyes. I was once a very quiet, reserved worshipper. I was scared to lift my hands in a church worship service. I was constantly concerned with what others thought and how I sounded. I could sing 17 songs in a row and yet not worship in spirit and truth for even a second.

But the more I studied God and His Word, all of that inhibition fell off of me. God was doing surgery on my heart. Now people describe my worship unto God as *free*—some say I'm like a wild woman, full of energy, always on my face, pure and uninhibited. That's why I carry a sound of freedom even when I'm silent; I carry Him everywhere I go. After all, where the Spirit of the Lord is, there is liberty! (See Second Corinthians 3:17.)

WHERE THE SPIRIT OF THE LORD IS, THERE IS LIBERTY!

Much is written in the Bible about David—David the shepherd boy, David and Goliath, David and Jonathan, King David, and many more David tales. Jesus and David carried a sound of freedom. What do I mean? Let's look at David's life more closely to see this sound. When David was a young boy out by himself in the fields tending to the sheep, he was also learning to fellowship with the Lord. He would write songs to God from his heart. He would write about the Lord and was obedient to pursue the Lord when no one was looking. It was just him and God every day and throughout the nights. The many psalms David wrote exude the sound of freedom and purity!

David was brought to play music before King Saul so the evil spirit that tormented the king would leave him. King Saul had no peace and he sought desperately to find someone who could relieve his agony. David's music was a sound of freedom not just for himself out on the backside of a hill worshipping before God—but now it was bringing freedom to the highest ruler in the land! David carried a sound of freedom and deliverance because he took the time to really know the Lord.

Later in his life David went into battle against many enemies and his heart and eyes stayed focused on God. David listened to God's voice, followed His commands, and gave God the glory; consequently, David was victorious time and time again. He praised with such abandon and with no thought to his dignity that he came right out of his kingly garments, meaning he put down all titles except one—worshipper of the one true God. David carried a sound of freedom and victory!

David sinned before God; he made bad choices to fulfill the lusts of the flesh. But when David realized his sin, he repented, turned from his ways, confessed humbly with a broken heart and contrite spirit before God, and prayed to have a clean heart and clean hands. David was being genuine, he carried the *sound of freedom and surrender!*

God said Himself that David was a man after His own heart! (See Acts 13:22.) That's a huge statement for God to make about someone who messed up and didn't always make the best choices; nevertheless, God marked David with that amazing legacy. Why? Because David released to God pure worship during his ups and downs—on the mountaintop and down in the valley. David's heart was for the Lord—and God, who searches all hearts, saw past David's shortcomings and saw the purity of his heart.

God knew David would release his sound and worship and praise unto God and he didn't care who was around or who saw. David didn't care if he looked undignified before the people; he cared more about carrying the sound of freedom! He carried God's glory! And the hand of God was upon him to do great things. Therefore, David's story has been told from generation to generation because he was marked with the sound of freedom.

David had a key to freedom and it was in his worship. Your freedom for your family and your life and your city is waiting on you to release your sound! This has nothing to do with singing well! It has nothing to do with playing an instrument well!

Remember the walls of Jericho didn't come down with a well-sung song or a band, they came down when the people obeyed God and shouted with a loud voice. There was something in their sound that caused physical, well-built walls to literally come crumbling down to the ground. (See Joshua 6.)

When was the last time you got alone and just began to cry out from your belly unto God and had the mindset like Jacob when he said to God, *"I will not let You go unless You bless me!"*? (See Genesis 32:26 NKJV.) Have you cried out to God, "Bless me, change me, transform me!"

You need one-on-One times with the Lord—times when you allow the power of the Holy Spirit to touch your life. Maybe you are reading this book but have never really experienced the Lord in a deep way. You can start today! You can literally tremble in His presence, not able to even say a word, but in that moment your sound of hunger goes forth. Tears hit the floor and the sound goes forth, and Your heart yearns so badly for the courts of the Lord it moves you to fall on your face and worship Him by laying down your own will, your dreams, your wants, your schedule, your ambition—your everything just to be with Him.

It's time to rip off the muzzle and begin to lift up your voice unto God. It's time to forget about how you look when you worship. That's why I covered the subject of identity before I wrote this part, because once you are established in the truth of who God really is and who you are in Him, then the opinions of others are broken off you, comparison is broken off, striving and working your way to Him is broken, and you live from a place of true rest.

Worship has been such an anchor for me. It is my anthem; I figured out a way to get to my Father's heart through worshipful surrender. I figured out a way to come out of hiding and break out of the chains through the sound of freedom worship. I pray the same breakthrough for you.

Prayer

Jesus, thank You for what You're doing in my life. At this point, I'm ready to release my sound from my heart unto You and into my atmosphere. I know that when I cry out to You, Your Word says You will deliver me—and so, Father, right now I cry out with my whole heart and I hold absolutely nothing back. I pray for holy boldness to release praise and prayers so You can be glorified and exalted. I command any fear that causes me to stay stuck or second guess Your will for me or causes me to shrink back to leave me right now in the mighty name of Jesus!

Declarations

I DECLARE in my life that I am free to lift my voice unto God (Judges 5:3; 2 Samuel 22:50; 1 Chronicles 16:23; Isaiah 51:11)

I DECLARE in my life that all bondage from my past will no longer hold me back (Psalm 27:6; Zechariah 2:10).

> I DECLARE in my life that I operate with a holy boldness (Psalm 57:9; Ephesians 5:19).
>
> I DECLARE in my life that my praise is a weapon (Isaiah 35:10; Jeremiah 51:48).
>
> I DECLARE in my life that I will shout unto God with a voice of triumph (Psalm 126:2; Jeremiah 31:7).
>
> I DECLARE in my life that I am chosen for such a time as this, in Jesus' name (Psalm 147:7; Revelation 15:3).

I invite you to take my *Seven-day Sound of Freedom Challenge.* These seven days of renewing of your mind and refocusing your heart on the things that bring transformation through the Word really help to shift you completely out of an old way of thinking or doing things. You begin to step into freedom more and more each day.

> ## YOU MAY BE FACING A BIG PROBLEM, BUT WE SERVE AN EVEN BIGGER GOD!

I encourage you to invite some friends to take the challenge with you or a home group or entire church. Set aside 14 days to really give yourself over to Jesus and watch breakthrough invade your life in a such a way that you end up *carrying* breakthrough with you everywhere you go rather than *needing* breakthrough everywhere you go!

SOUND OF FREEDOM
CHALLENGE

DAY 1

DAY OF THANKSGIVING

Scripture Focus

*Give thanks in all circumstances; for this
is God's will for you in Christ Jesus.*
1 THESSALONIANS 5:18

The Bible says in Psalm 100:4 to enter into God's gates with thanksgiving. As we go into the deeper things of God, the first thing we do at the gate is to give thanks. This seems simple, but something powerful is released into the atmosphere when you give thanks in all circumstances—even though you may be in a bad situation or going through a trial.

Thank God for what He has done, is doing, and will do in your life. Thank Him for the situation, because you will have a testimony of victory, God will be glorified, and you will experience the joy of being refined. Thank Him because you understand now that the Bible says *all* things are working for your good (see Romans 8:28), and you *believe* that *all things are working for your good!* And now you will stop doubting and fearing because you know God is true to His Word.

This day let no complaint or negativity about any situation come out of your mouth. Even if someone brings it up and tries to get you to rehearse the issue, change the conversation to one of thanking God. Say out loud, "Today I'm going to trust that my God is still on the throne and I thank Him that He has heard my prayers and is in the process of working it all out for my good." The road to freedom must start in your heart and mind and spirit. You must change the way you talk and proclaim and think. Remember, life and death are in the power of the tongue, so choose your words wisely.

Morning Prayer

This morning I lift up thanks to You, my God, because You are great and greatly to be praised! I thank You, Lord, for Your steadfast love and mercy toward me and all concerning me. Thank You, Lord, for what You have done in my life—You have brought me out of so many bad circumstances, and I remember Your faithfulness today. Thank You for what You are currently doing; even though I may not see the entire plan, I know that my steps are ordered and You are directing my path. And Lord, I thank You for what You are going to do in my life; and in this situation, I stand on Your Word that all things are working for my good. You love me and I love You, Father, and I'm called according to Your purpose!

Declarations

I declare today that my heart and mouth will lift up thanks all day to my God and I will guard my heart with His peace. I declare that the sound of freedom is in my thanksgiving today, in Jesus' name.

Nighttime Reflection

List 8-10 things or people you are thankful for:

_____

_____

_____

_____

_____

_____

_____

_____

_____

_____

DAY 2

A DAY OF RENEWING YOUR MIND

Scripture Focus

Do not conform to the pattern of this world, but be transformed by the renewing of your mind.
—ROMANS 12:2

Today our entire focus is about renewing our minds! We do this by getting into God's Word and allowing the Holy Spirit to bring it to life in our spirits so it can literally transform our lives! The Bible tells us to put off our old self and to be renewed in the spirit of our minds. Don't just speed-read through God's Word to see if you can really read it all, take time to pick out some Scripture passages and meditate on each verse. Look up the passage in other Bible translations and compare, pray on them, go back to them and reread to see if you get any new insight. Each time you do, your mind is being renewed and refreshed. Read

God's Word for one purpose—not for breakthrough or favor or blessing—to *know Him more* intimately. His favor and blessing are poured out when have more revelation of who He is. His word is a lamp unto our feet and a light unto our path (see Psalm 119:105).

Set aside some time today to meditate on a few Scripture verses and pray that the Holy Spirit will give you revelation of the Word and reveal to your heart all that He wants to teach you. Throughout the day, read the verses again and just let each word soak in. This is good to do every day to really grow in grace and truth! Share your favorite Scripture passages with your friends who may be doing this challenge with you. Listen to them as they tell you about their favorite verses and discuss what the Lord is revealing about His Word.

Morning Prayer

Thank You, my Father, for another amazing day in You. Teach me Your Word and reveal Your truth to my heart. As I meditate on Your Word today, God, let it come alive in my spirit and have the power to transform my old self into my new nature in You. Father, if I have any teachings or doctrines that are not from You, uproot them out of my spirit and replace them with the Gospel of truth. I know that You are with me today and I am being made new in You. In the mighty name of Jesus, I pray. Amen.

Declarations

I DECLARE today that my mind is being renewed by the Word of God and the power of the Holy Spirt. I have the mind of Christ, in Jesus' name!

I DECLARE that the sound of freedom is in the renewing of my mind.

Nighttime Reflection

Write out the Scripture(s) God laid on your heart today. Memorizing it will make it even more real in your life.

DAY 3

A DAY OF CONFESSION

Scripture Focus

*If My people who are called are by My name
will humble themselves, and pray and seek
My face, and turn from their wicked ways,
then I will hear from heaven, and will
forgive their sin and heal their land.*
—2 CHRONICLES 7:14 NKJV

We are going to have a day of searching our hearts and allowing the Holy Spirit to enlighten anything we may need to give to God. Whether it's control or fear or rebellion, offense, unforgiveness, or any number of personal issues, it's time to let go. *"If we confess our sins, [God] is faithful and just and will forgive our sins and purify us from all unrighteousness"* (1 John 1:9). We know God's grace abounds, but I also believe that a heart posture of repentance keeps us in a humble place before Him and allows the Holy Spirit to purify our hearts.

In my prayer time when I think about it or am prompted by the Holy Spirit, I will ask the Lord to forgive me of anything I'm aware of or unaware of that is not in alignment with His will. The Lord loves a broken and contrite spirit, and He will not despise it.

In your prayer time and throughout the day, ask the Holy Spirit to bring to light anything at all that needs to be revealed in your heart. As things come to your mind, be careful not to allow a root of condemnation to come in. Take whatever comes up and give it to God, confess it, and immediately receive His grace and forgiveness from His shed blood and move forward in His acceptance and love. There is no need to make yourself feel extremely bad or punish yourself somehow—His blood made the way for you to come boldly to His throne of grace!

Morning Prayer

Father, I come to You and praise You for my life that's hidden in You. Lord, search my heart today and see if there is any wicked way within me. Lead me in Your ways, God. I confess _____ (name whatever comes to mind) and I give it to You right now. I receive Your grace and mercy in this area of my life. Father, I know that You want to heal my wounded spirit and restore me, so I confess everything that I'm aware of and unaware of that is not in alignment with Your will—right now let it be gone, in Jesus' mighty name.

Declarations

I DECLARE in the name of Jesus that every hidden place in my life is brought to the light so I can walk in the mercy and love of my Almighty Father!

I DECLARE today that the sound of freedom is in my confession unto God.

Nighttime reflection

Read Psalm 51 and reflect on David's confession and his heart.

DAY 4

A Day of Soaking

Scripture Focus

One thing I have asked of the Lord, this only
do I seek: that I may dwell in the house of the
Lord all the days of my life, to gaze on the beauty
of the Lord and to seek him in his temple.
—PSALM 27:4

Some people say it's not polite to stare, but in this situation written about in Psalm 27:4, it is absolutely okay to stare or gaze or behold the Lord. We will spend today taking time to reflect on Him and think about His beauty, His majesty, His goodness, and all His amazing attributes. Even in the busyness of our lives, let's commit our hearts to taking time to stop to adore Him and let His beauty soak into our spirits.

In your prayer and devotion time, take a few quiet minutes and close your eyes to gaze on Him. Soaking to me is like taking a dry cloth and immersing it in a sink full of water. The cloth absorbs into its fibers as much of the water as possible until it's saturated with water and is dripping wet. Likewise, I want to be immersed in His presence just like that cloth and watch Him take over ever area of my life until Jesus comes out everywhere I go.

We discussed David, noting he had many accomplishments—he was a king, won many battles, defeated Goliath, was rich and popular, etc. But when he wrote Psalm 27:4, David asks the Lord for just *one thing,* one thing he would seek above all else—to be in God's presence and to gaze upon His beauty! Wow, no wonder God said David was a man after His own heart. When we set our hearts on seeking God and desiring Him above all the other things of this life and in this world, His hand of favor rests upon us.

Morning Prayer

Heavenly Father, I praise You this morning because You are such a good, good Father to me! Today, Lord, I'm asking You to show me who You are and allow me to gaze on You and see Your glory. I thank You that You are faithful to give to those who ask and knock and seek. My Lord, Your majesty and beauty are amazing and your faithfulness reaches to the sky. I open my heart to soak You into my spirit, heart, and mind. Help me to turn my eyes on You throughout this day. In Jesus' mighty name, amen.

Declarations

I DECLARE today that I will behold the Lord in all His beauty and know His goodness and grace and glory this day in the name of Jesus.

I DECLARE that the sound of freedom is found only in His presence.

Nighttime Reflections

Play some instrumental worship music with no lyrics and set your thoughts and heart on the Lord tonight.

DAY 5

A Day of Decrees

Scripture Focus

You will decree a thing, and it will be established
for you; and light will shine on your ways.
—Job 22:28 NASB

The definition of "decree" is an official order issued by a legal authority. As Christians and believers in Christ, we have the name of Jesus as the authority in our lives. You've been believing God for some things in your life, and today we actively stand up in faith and decree into our situation that His will be done on earth like it is in heaven! The Bible says in Proverbs 18:21 that death and life are in the power of the tongue, and those who love it will eat its fruit.

Today we focus on decreeing by the name of Jesus the promises of God over our lives. When you pray and decree, you speak them out in faith and don't waver. You trust that God is the mighty, powerful God and He is bigger than anything you are facing.

Today we aren't coming to God asking with a bit of fear in our voices and hearts. We aren't saying, "God, I ask for healing…only if it's Your will." No. He told us that by His stripes He has healed us and He told us not to expect anything if we come asking without believing. So, we decree His will that has already been made known, or declared, and we believe in faith that He is faithful to hear us. (See First John 5:14.)

When you go through your day today, decree His will on your job, in your community, your home and family, your mind. Even though you may not see it or feel anything, an official order has just gone out—and it was sent with authority, in the name of Jesus. We should be decreeing in accordance with His will only. Don't decree someone to be fired or that you will find a million dollars today (although that would be nice). Pray what you know is the heart of God, that aligns according to His will.

Morning Prayer

Father, I love You and I praise You for Your mighty hand and loving heart toward me today. I ask that the Holy Spirit leads and guides me into all truth, in the mighty name of Jesus!

Declaration

I DECLARE that the sound of freedom is in my decrees through the name of Jesus.

Decrees

I DECREE today that God is good and His mercy endures forever (1 Chronicles 16:34,41; Psalm 118:1; Jeremiah 33:11).

I DECREE today that I am a child of God and a co-heir of Christ (John 1:12; Romans 8:17).

I DECREE today that my family is saved and filled with God's Spirit (Acts 4:31; 13:52; Ephesians 5:18).

I DECREE today that I lack for nothing and God supplies all my needs according to His riches in glory (Nehemiah 9:21; Luke 22:35; Philippians 4:19).

I DECREE today that my mind is sound and God's perfect love has cast out all fear (2 Timothy 1:7; 1 John 4:18).

I DECREE today that I am free and free indeed; all bondage is broken off me in the name of Jesus (John 8:36; Micah 6:4; Romans 8:15).

I DECREE today that I'm blessed and highly favored everywhere I go (Genesis 22:18; Luke 1:28)

I DECREE today that the love of God abounds in my heart and I walk in love (2 Thessalonians 1:3; Deuteronomy 11:22).

I DECREE today that joy is my portion and any spirit of heaviness is lifting up and away from me, in Jesus' name (Nehemiah 8:10; Ecclesiastes 9:9; Isaiah 61:3).

I DECREE that my past is thrown into the sea of forgetfulness never to be remembered again (Micah 7:19; Psalm 25:18).

I DECREE that I use godly wisdom in all I say and do and that others see the light of Jesus in me (James 1:5; Matthew 5:16).

I DECREE that any attack that has been sent against me or my family comes to a halt now in the mighty name of Jesus (Isaiah 54:17; 2 Corinthians 10:4).

I DECREE that there is peace in my place of work and I will let my light shine there (1 Samuel 25:6; Romans 12:18; 2 Corinthians 13:11).

I DECREE that my life, my family, my finances, my ministry, and my body are all being restored by the power of the Holy Spirit (Job 42:10; Acts 3:21).

Nighttime Reflection

Write three major things you are believing God for and decree His Word over each one.

_____

_____

_____

_____

_____

_____

_____

_____

_____

DAY 6

A DAY OF CONSECRATION

Scripture Focus

*Therefore, I urge you, brothers and sisters, in
view of God's mercy, to offer your bodies as a
living sacrifice, holy and pleasing to God—
this is your true and proper worship.*
—ROMANS 12:1

Today is our day to purpose in our hearts to give ourselves
solely to God and to be living sacrifices for Him. We know
that we are called as His sons and daughters and share in His
inheritance, so we willingly covenant with God that our lives
now belong to Him. We stand before Him boldly because of
His blood, and we stand holy because of His finished work on
the Cross.

Verbally express to the Lord that you are solely His and He
can use you any way He wants for His glory. Being consecrated
simply means to be solely set apart for something and dedicated

to it. So although you may have been a Christian for years and years, it's good to express your heart of consecration to the Lord and commune with Him about it.

Consecration today may lead you to fast and pray for others. Or you may want to set aside some extra time to spend with the Lord in worship and praise or just sit quietly in His presence. However you choose to consecrate yourself before the Lord, I urge you to follow the leading of the Holy Spirit. Don't do things out of striving or performance or religious practices. Express genuine love and adoration for your heavenly Father. You may want to take Communion in your home or with your group of friends who are on this challenge with you, or have a worship night in your church or home group. Make it a time of being 100 percent focused on the Lord. You can revisit previous days that may come to mind as needing additional reflection.

Morning Prayer

Father, I honor and adore You today. I thank You for all You will reveal to my heart as I set this day aside to be consecrated unto You. Lord, I offer up to You my life. I freely give over my will and emotions, my wants, dreams, and plans and ask you to take them and make them into what You want. You are my God, my Father, my Lord, my Friend, my Strong Tower, and there is no other place I want to be than in Your will for me. Father, if there is anything in my life that has priority over You, please pull it down and take it away. I want You to reign sovereign in my life—fully and completely. In the precious name of Jesus, amen.

Declarations

I DECLARE in the name of Jesus that I will be a living sacrifice to the Lord and I will be holy and pleasing to Him in all that I do and say.

I DECLARE that the sound of freedom is in my consecration to God.

Nighttime Reflections

Write a list of things in your life that you willingly place in His care today.

_____

_____

_____

_____

_____

_____

_____

DAY 7

A DAY OF PRAISE AND CELEBRATION

Scripture Focus

Therefore I tell you, whatever you ask for in prayer, believe that you have received it, and it will be yours.
—MARK 11:24

Today is our day of absolute praise and celebration! You may be thinking, *But Jenny, I didn't get my miracle or breakthrough yet.* Let me give you a key truth—when you prayed for it, you believed in faith. This Scripture in Mark 11 tells us to believe that we already received the miracle or the thing we were asking for, and when we do, it will be ours.

So if you are praying for your prodigal child to come home, think to yourself, *How would I act right now if my child was home, saved, filled with the Holy Spirit, and serving the Lord?* You wouldn't be crying and stressing over it, you would have a smile on your face, possibly tears of pure joy, an extra pep in your step and a whole lot of praise on your lips. So what are you waiting for? Go ahead and begin to genuinely shout for the victory in faith that you have already received it—God has heard your cry and He will answer you.

You praise Him today because the victory is yours! He went before you and fought the battle already! Shake off any discouragement or bad news or negative report and put on some praise music and lift up those hands. Celebrate throughout this day!

One of my favorite stories in the Bible is found in Second Chronicles 20:1-30. It is about Jehoshaphat and the Israelites when they were about to face a huge army that could easily have killed them off. Jehoshaphat appointed men to sing to the Lord and praise God for His holiness. As they began to sing, the Lord set ambushes against the enemy who ended up killing themselves and the battle was won! Likewise, your battle is won by your praise and faith in your Father!

Morning Prayer

Father God, I give You praise for You are mighty and mighty to save. You never leave me or forsake me. Father, thank You for giving me the victory! Lord, I shout out Your name and Your great works to the heavens. You have overcome the world, Jesus, and I overcome because I'm hidden in You. Lord, all the glory and praise belong to You. You have done it again and again, and I set this day aside to lift up praise and celebrate all you've done and will do in the mighty name of Your Son, Jesus.

Declarations

I DECLARE today in the name of Jesus that the battle is won in my life by the blood of Jesus.

I DECLARE that Jesus is worthy of all the praise for the victory I'm now walking in.

I DECLARE that the sound of freedom is in my praise!

Nighttime Reflection

Write your praises to God. Also write or discuss with your group some changes you have experienced during this seven-day challenge.

I have participated in this challenge with a group of believers and it really does reposture your heart before God—even if you already walk very closely with Him. I encourage you to challenge yourself as many times during the year as you feel led, and each time you will see results because its focus is not on your big problems—it's on your bigger God!

Currently I travel and lead worship and teach people all around the world. One constant in my life, one thing I seek continually is to daily interface and fellowship with God the Father, Jesus the Son, and the Holy Spirit. God isn't just a small portion of my day in the morning or at night before bed or just on Sunday mornings—He is engraved into every minute of every day of my life for eternity.

You didn't just pick up this book by mistake. I believe that the Lord led you to read these words so you could hear Him speak directly to your heart about what who He is and who you truly are called to be in Him.

What Sound Do You Carry?

We all carry a sound. Some of us have carried a sound of defeat and sorrow for too long. Maybe your sound has been muted by the cares of this life and years of struggle. Or maybe you are just now discovering that you do have a sound and are learning to submit it to God and release it.

Please know that I hear the freedom bells ringing over you now. You are called for great and mighty things in the Kingdom of God. Today I say over you that whatever you have been walking through, there is true freedom in Jesus that you will not find anywhere else.

My life was almost wiped out by the enemy, and at times all looked hopeless and I felt like a lost cause. Even after I was saved, it sometimes seemed life was too much of a mess to matter. But God's plans for me were set into motion and I'm thankful He was pursuing me even in my most messed-up times. He wanted to show me that He is the only true Father who can love His children unconditionally. Now each day I get to see and know Him more and more and in new and different ways.

> NEVER GIVE UP ON YOUR DREAMS OR WHAT YOU'VE BEEN PRAYING ABOUT.

Never give up on your dreams or what you've been praying about. I wouldn't be here today if I would have gave up the first time someone in church talked about me or hurt my feelings. But in my daily surrender, God began to show me that my life wasn't my own and that the freedom I carried needed to go forth and be shared. So I had to choose to not be offended or hurt over things people do. That's one of the most important lessons and longest-to-learn lessons I have had to work on. But once that revelation really hit my spirit, it was a game changer for me.

I've heard it said that "Dead people aren't offended." I can't be offended either because I'm not living for what pleases me or bothers me or how things affect me. My eyes are on my God and

I've learned to rest in Him and be led by Him. Am I perfect in this attitude? No, I'm not. But I'm growing daily in grace and truth and I've learned that even if I mess up and miss it, I can *immediately* run to my Father—not run away in shame. I can be reconciled and led in the right direction without condemnation. That's a pretty amazing life, if you ask me—to constantly have a good Father right beside me every step of the way and lovingly correcting and shaping and molding me into who He wants me to be. I wouldn't want it any other way.

When writing this book, the Lord put it in my heart to make sure that I left room for a call to salvation because I believe He knows there will be those who read it but haven't truly given their life to Him or maybe they did a long time ago but walked away. Maybe that is you and now you're reading this and God is tugging on your heart because He wants you to come home.

He has been calling your name, pursuing you with His everlasting love, and no matter what mess you may or may not be in right now, you can be His child and ask Him into your heart. Don't let fear or shame make you pass this moment by. Jesus said if anyone comes after Him, that person must choose to follow Him. Today, surrender your life to Him.

Say in your heart now or out loud that you need Jesus to take over. Give Him your life and choose to follow Him this day. Believe that He is Lord and call on Him. His Word says that whoever calls on the name of the Lord shall be saved! So glory to God, I rejoice with you if you prayed for Jesus to be your Lord and that you will now follow Him.

This life is a blessing and a gift from God. We have lasting breakthrough and victory in every situation; and nothing, *nothing*, is too big for our God! Allow the sound of freedom to be loud over your life today and every day.

ABOUT THE AUTHOR

Jenny Weaver is a wife and homeschool mother. She believes in building families and communities in the Kingdom of God. She is best known for "Singing the Scriptures" live each week on her Facebook page. Hundreds of thousands of people worldwide view her page every week and share their testimonies of how their lives have changed since watching Jenny sing the Scriptures.

Transformed by God's renewing power, Jenny's heart is to lead people into an encounter with the Holy Spirit that will transform them as well.

Jenny believes that worship led in Spirit and in truth with a pure heart and no limitations ushers in God's glory, which invades the earth! It is Jenny's desire to lead prophetic and spontaneous high praise worship that releases the song of heaven into the hearts of all humanity!

"I'm amazed at the hand of God on my life."
—JENNY WEAVER